Cat's Whisker

PHILIP GROSS

Cat's Whisker

ff

faber and faber

LONDON · BOSTON

First published in 1987 by
Faber and Faber Limited
3 Queen Square London WC1N 3AU
Reprinted 1988

Typeset by Goodfellow & Egan, Cambridge
Printed in Great Britain by
Redwood Burn Ltd
Trowbridge Wiltshire

© Philip Gross, 1987

British Library Cataloguing in Publication Data

Gross, Philip
Cat's whisker
I. Title
821'.914   PR6057.R5/

ISBN 0–571–14894–8
ISBN 0–571–14895–6 Pbk

Contents

Acknowledgements

With thanks to the editors of: *Acumen, Agenda,* BBC *Poetry Now, Encounter, The Green Book, Lancaster Festival Anthology 1984, Listener, Literary Review, National Poetry Competition Prizewinners 1985, London Magazine, Observer, Orbis, Outposts, P.N Review, Poetry International (US), Poetry Review, Prospice,* Schools Poetry Association *Footnote, Scripsi, She, South West Review, Times Literary Supplement, Vision On.*

Cat's Whisker‑‑

'Cat got your tongue?'
Go on, I thought, *laugh!* (They did.) *She
understands.* Charmer and snake in one,
she padded in and coiled beside me.

I could talk to her,
with her lithe knowing silences,
no questions asked, only the whurr
of a finely-tuned apparatus

idling. 'Is it true?'
I whispered. 'You see ghosts?' She seemed
to smile. (Then again, cats always do.)
But the family's day-long 'atmospheres'

pained her: that slow build
and itch of static in grown-up altitudes
above my head. She flexed. Yawned. Bristled.
We were bad music to her. Yes, she knew

what wavelengths lace the air.
But how? The first twitch of her whiskers
was the sign. She'd be stroked anywhere
but there. *Cat's-whisker*: the encyclopaedia

showed a crystal set, a family
bent close. *Cack-rackle-hiss*: a jumbling
rush of atmospherics . . . Then, haltingly
at first, this small voice, coming through.

[1]

Revelations

It should have been the glassy sea
where seraphim cast down their crowns
or something. It was stone. I was thirteen.
Something *had* to change, so why not now,

my first Communion? As the gloomy swell
of the organ washed me to the altar rail
I glimpsed her, kneeling; how her sensible
shoe gaped back a little from her heel

which was white and thin. I tried to equate
the polystyrene wafer gummed to the roof
of my dry mouth with any earthly taste,
with any bread or body that I knew.

I stared at the polished marble till my eyes
mazed, and it was the surface of a pond,
tensed. Slow mud-swirls began to rise
like clouds about to part, beneath, beyond.

Loving Spoonful

Over the top they go, the do-or-die brigade.
They fall in their thousands, feebly threshing.
The fittest go bludgeoning on. They spread
like spilt milk from a moment's indiscretion.

They're a smear on the microscope slide.
Wipe it clean. So much for . . . was it lust
or a righteous going-forth-to-multiply?
What sort of God whips in this Exodus,

what grizzle-thighed games-master hacking *Go
for it, lads!* from the touchline?
                                                    No,

it's us, the love we make. Or think we do.
It makes us, using me, love, using you.

Post Marks

1 A SNOW SCENE

The stamp brags: *Salyut* girdling the earth
with flags and red tape. *Two weeks in the air?*
the postmark whispers, *On whose desk?* Beneath,
the address argues from general to particular:
state, city, street (as cameras might zoom in
on hundred-yard irregularities from space)
to a number and a name. Inside, a snow scene
and a New Year's greeting:
                              'PEACE.

Good news. Our Vovka is come home.
Is better. We walk a little out today
in Progress Park. Each twig bears snow,
its own load. (See, the camera tells no lie!)
All earth is held still, even the stream.
There are bright bubbles in the ice.
He stands, I stand, till we are numb,
not to disturb. We hope for peace.'

Can that be all? This game of patience
is her life. *Better? Home?* No clerk in uniform
trusts words less. *Camera? Lie?* She means more
than she says. *Peace? Numb?* We'll shake
it out of her . . .
        'What is there left to hide?'
she shrugs. *'What do you want me to say?*
It's better, better. Can it be denied?'

2 FROM THE OTHER SIDE

'It's a quiet life.
I play myself at chess
turning the board each move
imagining a deathless
master opposite, say
Alekhine
        though Alekhine
nearly did for me
in '44 (after your time).
Some Youth League cub
doing his good deeds mistook
my Alekhine's *Der Kampf*
for quite another book.
I was frogmarched off.
By luck the commissar
was a player, of sorts.
He kept me all night there
at a trestle table in a room
without windows. Doors
clanged to, feet clicked
and I glimpsed corridors.
I played my best ever:
I let him win. Towards dawn
he shouted "You don't *try*!"
A sacrifice, I swore. And won.
He shook my hand: "We play
again. After the war."

[5]

More often, though,
I try to guess what your
moves might have been.
I never had your flair.
You'd sacrifice the lot;
you'd break through or
be damned. I was the plodder
and glad of a draw,
the quiet life.

               So here
I sit, the last of us,
on the edge of my world,
staring out across
the State Farm's great
wide-opened squares
of wheat. Or give the dead
another game. Where
in the world are you?
Did you really break through?
And would I post this,
could I, if I knew?'

3 ENGLISH AS A FOREIGN LANGUAGE

'Dear Sir,
          You will not know me but I wish you to.
I study English two years. How I wish for some one
I may correspond to. Mother says this might
to be "misunderstood". I know in other's tongue
are so many things I may not say. But I shall use
a dictionary. Why should not peoples to each other write?

Here see my photograph. The Upper School Work Unit
at the Heroes of October State Farm. Last left at back
besides the many potatoes, he in the spectacle is me.
I am not strong in sport. And some time I am sad
for the brothers and sisters I have not. I am unique.
I keep old things, as stamps. I save small countries

that are not now. (May I cut off your Queen's head
if you write?) Also I have Grandfather's red and white
chess men though I play not; a boar's tusk, a accordian,
a bullet from the Patriotic War, a piece of meteorite
that Father sent me (my best treasure) from Siberia.
He labours in important projects, and is long gone.

Please write, if it is permitted. Tell me of your
own self. And please teach me a good idiom to startle
my teachers. For I confess, my grades are poor.
I could not live in English. You can say too many little
different things. Here it is simpler. Where *you* have four
or five words, some time we have none at all . . .'

[7]

The Balance

for Helen

It narrows down to us
or so it seems. Grafting your tree
to mine the genealogist makes history
   converge to a precarious
   balance: man and wife,
yours/mine, left/right. Even that patch
gone threadbare on each side . . . We match
   the frayed ends, life
   for life, Gentile for Jew.
What separated Abraham, packed west
from Riga on a slow train (all the rest
   implied: *d.1942*)
   from Karl (*d.1943*)
whose line went east to peter out somewhere
beyond Irkutsk? A few miles, then a war.
   My enemy's enemy . . .
   can't quite make them friends
though the difference between one cattle truck
and another is as hindsight, history or luck
   dictates. So much depends.
   The only point of balancing
is us. 'He who preserves one soul,' teased old
Maimonides, 'is as one who preserves the world.'
   If each equates with everything,
   how do we count? I'm afraid,
my love, if there's a balance it won't be
the kind we *keep*, but that in which we
   hang, and shall be weighed.

Baltic Amber

It's a drop from a tall well of light
in a forest of vertical shadows, a resinous
   stillness. It's warm to the touch
in my palm, at your throat; hospitable to us

   as to the ant, older than Christendom,
preserved in its sweet pine sap. Where are
   the hordes of Tartary, the Knights
Of The Teutonic Order, Wallenstein, the Tsar?

   Wear it close, night and day, a charm
against history. It takes nothing to heart:
   flipped up on the tideless shingle,
scavenged for a hoard, for booty; bartered,

   a gewgaw to the broad and brilliant
piazzas of the south. Then clutched in flight
   by a dark-haired child, in crowds,
on platforms, cobbles, quays. Crossing by night

   see her sleep; the ship creaks
swaying like a forest and her fingers, thin
   as a grandmother's, clutch the stone
like life. Tonight it lies against your skin.

A Breton Dance

A stone grey town with a name like a bell:
Tinténiac. Was this the place? The time?
The square was empty, blinkered for the night.
On, out beyond a hoarding *ZONE INDUSTRIELLE*

we drove between vacant Euro-factories,
beached white whales. And this was it:
a lorry-park like a floodlit airstrip,
and the dancers. Then the bark and wheeze

of the *bombarde* cut the hubbub, keen
as bad cider. The shock of it flowed
among them, losing young and old
in a pattern of spirals, yet a single line.

A hundred heel-and-toes became one long
slow shudder, like a snake down all its scales.
We backed away. It flexed its coils.
The pipe throbbed round and round and on

into the night, needling, defying rhyme,
reason, development or cure: the sweet ache
of dreaming yourself a nation. When you wake
the place is always wrong. That, or the time.

Hole in the Ground

DELABOLE

New times, new voices, pebble-dash on slate
– what's it to me? I'm passing through
now like those strangers on the trim estate
that was Lobb's field. Yes, but I know
that snicket at the lane's end, and I let
it lead me, back, to what the cottages
conceal. I duck the DANGER sign to edge

close, closer . . . *Whack*, and jackdaws sheer
off scolding across half a mile of emptiness.
I almost catch the ricketing of winding gear,
the shudder and whump of a blast. Almost.
They dug a small mountain out of here
and camped in the slag: sullen, swart,
close as one slate to t'other, short

of shank and temper; drunk, a *pestilence*
to good farm folk, till a lonely Methodist
unfurled damnation. A mutinous silence.
Then one voice, a slow joke: *Mister,*
we ben in the Pit a long time since.
A dropped stone, rousing to a grim
accord of heroes, a Revival hymn.

*

We expect them, fervently: the saints
those stern tremendous men
with eyes like boreholes, waterfalls of beard,
a steady hand
to split souls cleanly at one blow.
They will descend
any day, in thunderclouds of steam
from the Great Western Railway, crying: Where
the pulpit? Where the text? *And we*
shall lead them to the quarry's edge.
Behold, the earth laid open at the page,
the difficult passage. They will make it clear.

*

In the slate museum
he's on show, preserved, the last.
He turns from me

to question the grain, his chisel tip
nosing the spot,
the mallet almost gentle in his fist.

He knocks. The slab
comes open crisply with a sigh.
He leans ajar

[12]

two perfect tablets as if I
        might read. Stooked
sheaves behind him, they recede

        to headstones packed
aslant in chapel plots; low slate
        scaled terraces

which darken under rain, roofs
        shivering to steel.
He stares back. Neither of us moves.

Time and Motion

'Arthur. *Mister* Arthur, lad.' His swivel chair
wheedled; he delicately plucked one hair
from his nostril. 'Let's have a bit of decorum.

Damn!' He swiped the phone up. 'What's that? See
mine of the 15th.' Slam. 'If it weren't for me
they'd be out of a job, those office johnnies.'

The warehouse exhaled damp and cardboard. 'Stores
consists of four sectors. Sectors, A, B, C and 4.
Each crate's got a code. Don't ask what they *are*,

it'll only confuse you. Time and motion! Eh?
"Tidy up"? Took YEARS to get it just this way
and you . . . I can see, you won't last long.

Trouble is, the young . . .' – he swirled his dregs
for my future – '. . . don't know how to *pace* theirselves.
Christ! The lorry's due. Look lively.'

The windows crawled with heat; the warehouse hummed.
I learned to prang bluebottles with the staple gun.
We backed into dark recesses, to *stocktake* . . .

'Well, well.' One mush of cardboard housed a frantic
sty of woodlice and, like dull brassy lipstick,
cartridges. 'Home Guard. By, takes you back.

[14]

Let's see.' He cramped one in the workshop vice,
gave me a hammer and a three inch nail: 'A nice
crisp tap. No, don't tickle it. *Hit* it.

Jesus! That'll show 'em.' My ears whinnied.
Outside, the rhododendrons thrashed, shaking free
a squad of pigeons. They cranked themselves off.

A slight blue ghost leaked from the spent case.
I rolled my tongue around its shocking taste
for weeks. Rain tom-tommed the tin roof

the day I gave my notice. 'University?' He shook
his head. 'You'll regret it. Read all the books
you like, you won't find a better hole than this

though mark my words, you'll try.'

Stonepecker

At the crack
of dawn a shadow slopes
up the lane to the quarry:
Old Jope.

Rack rack.
What's that kickstarts
like the whack and trip
of a dicky heart?

A snuff of smoke.
A burnt stone smell.
Rackatack bashes on
like a pecker in Hell.

Gone broke:
no copper no zinc no coal.
Got the richest vein of nothing
in a county full of holes.

Behind his back
it's *Old Man Jope got no hope*
  Scrubs his face with a stone for soap
  Tied the knot with a length of rope . . .

No joke.
He had a missus who nobody saw.
He let her out once
in 1954.

She ran amuck
in Plymouth, ran off with a sailor.
He's been digging ever since.
Going to catch them in Australia.

Come unstuck.
The vicar came enquiring for his soul.
Damned if he could find it.
Must have lost it down the hole.

Got the quack
up from Bodmin to examine his head.
It was granite to the core
with a little trace of lead.

There's the shack
where he sits in tumbledown weather.
Stone dust and diesel grease
hold it together.

Take a peek.
Hush. The *rackatack* stops.
You can hear claws click
when a jackdaw hops.

Lob a brick
down the lifelong drop. Quick
run
run away and don't look back

'cos the stonepecker's after you
                              CRACK!

Moore

unnh   grunnh?   grohh
wassamatter? Wh'am I? Who the? No
go'way. I was dreaming. I was deep.
Where was I? Dancing. Arm in arm in . . . *She.*
All round me. We were waltzing, slow
slow, round and round. And suddenly
there's all this . . . *unstuff.* Is it sky?
I never asked. *You* did this to me
damn you. You made me this: I

am. But I can take it. Mass-
culine, I ham, a bullwork. Charlie Atlas
torse, the strangth of clunched hands,
nubbled biceps (feel that!) in a man-
to-manly buddy-hug.
                But mateless,
muzzlebound, manhandling . . .
unthings. Unnh. A not-
hole in the heart. *You*, you abandoned
me, you left me wanting . . . what?

[18]

The words gro wrong. It's a terribore
think, this onliness, this wanting . . . *more*.
There must be others, no? No eyes to see,
I not-quite-touch them, close. Quick flimsy
curious things, warm breaths.
                                    I'm floored,
yes down but no not out – a lourdly
drunk who might yet lurge upright, embrace
the emptiness and astonish the dance-floor
with a coup of (how to put it?) grace.

Questions, Questions

'And where do you think you're off to? What's the meaning of it? What about your breakfast?' A thin drift of midges rose around him, tacky little touch-prints on his skin. He flapped them away. *'Well? Speak up.'*

He stooped for a stone and flung it wide into the trees. There was a shrill and fluster of small birds.

They would have to wait. When he got home, he'd have an answer then. Or rather, no, he wouldn't. He would look down; hot bafflement would rise in him like milk boiling over, and he would squirm and mutter, and what would be the sense of it? So at last, merciful heavens, they would lose patience. Having won, they would let him be. *'There, you see! You don't know what to say.'*

The track wound a contour through the woods. Here a granite sleeper lay bedded, notched twice where the rails had run. There, a granite gatepost, bleeding rust from the hinge. He scuffed on. Gatepost? Why a gatepost? And his mind stopped there, though his body pushed on, vacantly.

Not that it mattered. But the track was suddenly going nowhere. There was an itch of unplaceable sadness. As if some total stranger was waving goodbye from a train, and there was no one on the platform but you. His feet slowed, stopped, turned. There was the post.

Prickly big-grained granite, blotched with lichen, it sank in bushes against rising ground. Just here, though, the texture of the undergrowth changed; through the leaves he glimpsed not the bank but more leaves. He pushed in a little. He pushed through.

He pushed out of the bush and into a deep pouch of shade. This was *somewhere else*. The bank rose behind him and closed round, steeper and stony-broken, round in a deepening bowl. A quarry. Ahead was the fifty-foot grey face, sheared off in tiers of small black overhangs. Beneath, it opened back and down into a greenish cave.

I'm alone, came a loud thought. Face to face. As if, he thought, as if it was waiting. Just for me. And he, and everything, was very still.

Nothing happened. Nothing ever does, he thought, not really. That took the edge off the strangeness and one step at a time, very gingerly, he picked through the loose slag and brambles, into the shadow of suspended tons of rock.

But it, whatever *it* was, wasn't there. The cave came to nothing. The roof dripped, dripped and glistened. It dipped to the ground, which was clutter furred with black moss and crested by a fern in improbable green. He backed, in a crouch, out, found a stone and sat. And sat.

He was hungry. Breakfast, he thought. Mum and dad. He flinched. Here it was quiet, no birdsong even, so quiet he could discern a faint high hum inhabiting the cave, like the hundred-year echo of the last pick stroke, the last rip and slump of stone, the clunk of couplings, and the lock chain on the gate.

The sun moved, and the shadows. Time was all awry. The hunger went, but he was suddenly embarrassed at his need to shit and he hunkered in the bushes watchfully, as if at any moment they might be there, guffawing: *Well, sod me, lads! What have we here?* The quarrymen, that is. That his parents might come, or the police, seemed quite fantastic. They'd never find him here. It wasn't on the map, he knew. It wasn't really anywhere.

Now there were no shadows. Things lost detail and pulled closer. Dusk began to silt the quarry up. A whole day's hunger griped him abruptly, dizzily. He had waited, hadn't he, and what had he got? Outside, nothing had changed. Mother and father. Questions. Supper. Search parties. Questions, questions. Supper. Bed. He'd got nothing, damn it! He picked up a nub of rock and flung it meanly. The *crack!* splintered round behind him. 'Damn you,' he repeated out loud, louder. And his voice rang, shocking, vibrant, given back to him in full, repaid with interest. And again, again. He burst out laughing and it all laughed with him, loud and long.

Tar Boilers

Sleepwalkers
wading in bright mist
or deep-sea divers
shuffling silt, they cuss
the dodgy burner.
First sun prinks the frost.

Each word becomes visible.

They crank
a handle and the dribbly
cauldron gulps. Volcanic
gloss-black slurry
nudges down the shute, rank,
steaming like fresh manure,

serviceable.

Now they tamp
a square plot. The roller
bumbles and clanks
and seams it matt.
The driver huffs and stamps.
A thermos steams in his mitt.

Cars cough awake.

A small boy waits,
the pavement quaking at his feet.
He buffs a bright
new-minted ha'penny:
1958.
Now? *Now!* He tweaks it in.

Signed, sealed. He runs away.

The Nearest Place
to Nowhere

No, it wasn't the smash of the waves below
    shook me upright in my bed
but a thud like a muffled drum, a slow
    dead march above my head.

'It's him,' Ned's voice was tight and grim.
    'Old Hallelujah Todd!
He's flipped his lid. He's talking to him-
    self and, worse, to God.'

As ginger then as a lighthouse mouse
    I crept. Sober or pissed
John Todd was strong as three of me.
    I saw the spanner in his fist,

I saw a shock of ripped-out wires
    a frost of shattered glass –
the radio . . . He saw me. Smiled.
    'Listen, boy. Peace at last.'

It was two months till relief fell due
    and twenty miles from shore.
Outside, two thousand miles of swell
    came beating at our door.

The wind-gauge wailed, a thumping gale
    rose mad as him within.
And two men sat as jumpy-still
    as flies in a biscuit tin.

[25]

A day and a night, a sleepless night.
    Up, down, outside and in
we heard him plod, keeping watch for God
    as we kept watch for him.

He nailed us there with a twitch of a stare.
    'Do you think *He* don't see
our dot-dash-dot in the darkness where
    He meant no light to be?

'And don't you smile . . .' His eyes cut bright.
    He stumped outside again.
And that's where we found him, sat upright
    face set to the carving rain.

He was drenched, chilled rigid, dead.
    We dragged him, Ned and I,
by the boots and the head. 'What now?' I said.
    'We can't just let him lie.'

It was the nearest place to nowhere.
    Half an acre of rock outside.
Not a crumb of soil to cover him.
    We waited till low tide,

then scuttled out. I pointed: 'Well?' –
    eyed Ned and Ned eyed me.
''Tis scarcely proper, but . . .' A hole.
    'Feet first, maybe?'

The tide and the wind had swung about.
   As solemn as we dared
we lowered him in. Then Ned wrung out
   his Book of Common Prayer.

I levered a boulder from its cleft
   and trundled it into place.
Ned bawled, 'The Resurrection and the Life!'
   The wind slapped it back in his face

and ripped the waves to a hard sleet spray
   that raked us as we stood.
We turned to run. Then a boom like a gun
   shivered us like rotten wood.

and the stone flipped up like a bottle top
   and there comes old John Todd,
punched up, head first, on a fist of foam
   going up to meet his God.

Well, it may have been a blow-hole,
   a trick of the turning tide,
a fluke of a tale like Jonah's whale,
but this I know: when it's time to go
   there's nowhere you can hide.

A Cornish Saint

They can't be serious, those two-a-penny saints
    washed up like holy jetsam: no mere boats
for them, but millstones, coffins, kegs. So delicate
    Saint Ia had to float
in on a leaf. Their visitations stopped abruptly

as the trippers' now. St Ives is emptied like a till
    and counted. Stiff winds scrub the town.
Summer timetables tatter and flap; awnings rattle
    up, are battened down
as the season stows itself away, no time for me

and precious little shelter. Ia's chapel on the cliff
    is padlocked and the path slips ledge
to ledge, nowhere to go but down, brittle thrift
    for handholds. At the edge
deep water thumps and swashes, almost within reach.

A wicked glitter underfoot . . . I'm not the first.
    Someone lugged bottles here and sat
and drank, and watched, and drank, with a thirst
    he couldn't fathom; then smashed
every last one. Green glass lapped him like the sea

and then? Was that *her* on the water as the tide-
    flow tightened to the point, as the Godrevy
light began to pry? *Oh pray for us, unauthorized*
    ridiculous Saint Ia, in these heavy
times. And did she beckon:

                  Come with me . . . ?

The Lookout

It's a rain-swabbed cell, niched high
   in a shale slab headland
   on a wrecking coast. Inside,
dark like the dark inside the eye.

It's a post not manned this century.
   Three arched windows
   west, south, east
take in the brilliant deceptions of the sea

in sunlight, or how it mulls the glow
   now as the snaggled shore
   beds down in shadow
Waves muster, sharpening the narrow

spit of black where one last fisherman
   shoulders his tackle to push
   up the steep scree path
to here. His breath drags. He stoops in

shucking his bag. He tastes the cool
   church smell of slate.
   Where he stood,
pale foamings pucker and spill

till there's nothing. And suddenly
   he's chilled. It's late.
   He should be going but
can't move. The long *hush* of the sea

[29]

has silenced him. A wink of light
   traces the coast road.
   Now it swivels, fans
up, up and seaward, as if taking flight.

Two Waters

This is the place. Water and water meet,
  one quick from the wide light
  of the moors, one slow from a deep-
shadowed combe. It's done in black and white,

fine threads of ink unravelling, an endless
  rip and slalom, gulps of foam
  backpedalling, sleeked lines of force
where the current sets its shoulder to the stone.

Who could pick up the stitches now? At the end
  the dash and slap of oils brought her
  no sense of 'being there'. She turned
to etching: sit, wait, watch the living water.

This is her place. Look too close and it takes
  you clean away. A boulder
  bucks and rides upstream against
the flow. The waters fold, and you are nowhere

much like her, whose hand smoothed the metal
  ready for the acid, wax and knife.
  The fingerprint of water . . . Still,
it seems to move. And never will, not in this life.

Everything Must Go

BUY! BUY! the sales cry, WHILE STOCKS LAST.
TWO FOR THE PRICE OF ONE! EVERYTHING
MUST GO. It's too much. Joan, going grey
by the minute, goggles. Crisp mannequins
return her stare. They give nothing away.

'Buck up!' There's a tug at her sleeve.
'Can't wait for ever.'
                        'Mother, please . . .'
Words fail her; they always do. 'Oh, why . . . ?'
Joan flounces free; the scrum heaves;
she's going under, with a small cry:

'Mother!'
                Hand finds hand.
'You lummock. God knows what you'll do
without me.' Mildly grumbling they shove
on home. Who would have chosen, who
could have planned this? Love

ropes them together like a punishment –
no, like plough horses, stony ground
spilling to tilth behind them: one
day at a time, the slow plod up, around
and back. It gets the living done.

From the Fast Train

The town falls by the wayside. Gone astray
in the urban outback, our racketing dulls
to an auctioneer's gabble. Rails splay
into rusty shuntings. Long grass rankles.
There's a rash of fireweed, smatterings of may

and there, gone feral on clinker, a shock
of lupins, wild colonials. Was that a goat
cropping the scrub beside a landlocked
quarter acre? Scratched earth and a rain-butt?
Thin smoke tippling from a corrugated shack

no path leads to or from? And who'd
be waiting there, who'd be at home
nursing a Coronation mug, tea stewed
to a metallic tang? Yes, that's him.
'Such a time,' he'd say. 'What kept you?'

Inter City

Between the embankment and the Pentecostal Hall
    there's a scrag-end of grass
with a slide like a watchtower. On a tangled
    swing, hugging its chains,
Tracey flips *Love's Raging Fires.*

                                              'Well?

What's it all about?' Sumitra's quizzical,
    side-saddle on the seesaw.
'Lot of fuss about nothing,' Tracey smiles.
    'Want it?'

                        'You're joking!
Think! My Dad . . .'

                              Tracey thinks. The rails

twitch, quicken to a tingling. And the Inter City
    whacks by, thistledown
whipped jiggling in the slipstream. It's half way
    to Birmingham (the wispy nothings
drifting down down) before Tracey speaks: 'Beats me.

What do your lot *do*?'

                              Sumitra shrugs. She tries
    the swing, first tentative,
then kicks away. Her peach silks flounce and rise,
    flare and descend, a gift
of wings, a kindling. There are fires and fires.

Little Dancer

She's stopped in her tracks, her face
up, eyes and lips
                    tight, braced
for what? Applause? A slap, more like.
Or a kiss from a dusty uncle?
                              Not in spite
but because of the ash-brittled lace
that frills her hips
                    she's irretrievably
exposed,
        betwixt and between,
                              not quite
a child, her body not quite dragooned into grace,
her stocking puckered at one knee . . .
She's very old,
              fourteen,
                        and cast in bronze.
Her plinth is wired. After we've gone
and the attendant snicks the lights out one
by one, a black box on the wall
considers her. It watches, all
night, as her mother might have done.

Tabernacle Yard

Strict and particular, dwindling
fiercely, they met *'8 p.m.*
God Willing' in a firebrick
kennel up a *cul-de-sac*
so tight to the railway's cinder
scarp they timed the Psalm –

The Lord reigns; let the earth quake;
let the people tremble . . . –
to contend with the 8.15.
Through narrow panes
they glimpsed the fireman's face
bent to his chink of Hell.

'So shall the world be borne away,
smoke streaming after fire,
the Romish temples, the gin palaces,
the music halls, the horseless
carriages. Thunder by night. Yea,
brothers, let us prophesy!'

The end is always nigh; theirs came
and went. The padlock on the gate
fat as a fobwatch clinks and swings.
A rusty block-and-tackle hangs
in chains. Wrecks *sans* wings, lights, chrome,
everything, our write-offs wait

for GOFF & SON, the resurrection
men who promise BODY WORK (beneath,
NO JOB TOO SMALL) but never seem
to come, except to underfeed
one sidelong mean Alsatian.
It smiles humbly, with its teeth.

The Private Sector

FABRICATIONS, the sign says, up an alley
that could be the scene of a crime.
The workforce has gone cannily
to ground. Whatever their business is
it's none of mine.
Under charked brick arches
on the quarter hour, each shed
fills with a labyrinthine
grumbling as a train crumps overhead.

Face up, spraddled beneath a van
there's a body in a boiler suit.
That monkey wrench might be the weapon.
But it's only oil
puddling beside him, and his foot
taps reggae, his mouth shapes the wail.
Head swollen with a Rasta tam, he's
wired to far-off sounds, deaf-mute
to the joiners' operatic agonies.

A power-saw whinges and stutters.
They're feeding the caged blade.
It digs in, slobbering, but is
wrestled free; it runs shrill.
The planks are clattered out and laid
to rest in the sun. The smell, still
warm, turns the mechanic's head.
He smiles. We've got it made.
It's simple as sliced bread.

A Glass, Darkly

The odd one, last of its set, subtly askew
   on its stem, it stood like 'best'
     in the cabinet, unused,
   set for the one, the uninvited guest.
Heirloom or jumble-trove, I never knew

but when the party palled and someone sniggered
   'Let's play séances', it came to hand
     as if called. Our giggles
   put a thrill in it; it quivered, and
was off. 'What's your name?' Doggedly it figured

gibberish to every question till: '*Is* anybody there?'
   With two fell swoops that nearly left all
     our fingers crooked in mid-air:
   N . . . O . . .
       They had their hoot, then called
for a new game. Huffed in a corner, I could only stare

into the glass. Its emptiness still held a darkening
   of red. I gentled it, stroking the rim. It
     stirred. Yes, through my finger,
   through my bones, it rose. The party hit
a hush. From somewhere way beyond us, it began to sing.

Oh

No one at home.
The goldfish bowl
was empty. It became
a crystal ball.

Not quite empty.
As I pudged my nose
to the glass, snow-flurries
of scurf-dust fell and rose.

Gran spoke. I shifted
focus: the bowl filled
with stray squints
of our world but pulled

inside out, the sofa
sucked like licorice
looping the grandfather
clock. 'It's like this,'

she said. 'When you've lived
a long time you get tired . . .
Believe me.' 'But where *is*
he? Now?' She sighed.

'There's a great pond, far
away . . . All his family
and friends are there.' 'Where?
Show me. Take me. Please!'

We went by bus. The garden
grew white stones in tidy rows
and a droopy fountain
tinkled. To, fro, to and fro

limp flicker-flames
of fish lapped dimly,
hundreds, all the same.
'But which? Which is he?'

I'd know my Glooper anywhere,
his blotchy bit . . . Wouldn't I?
'No one has blotches here.
Washed clean. Isn't that nice?'

They grazed our shadows, quite
indifferent, mouthing *Oh.*
Oh.
        'No!' I cried.
'Take me home. Please. Take me home!'

Grandmother's Footsteps

Stoke up the fire.
She was not to be gainsaid.
Brushing words aside
her hand stubbed *There!*
and *There!* She made
us understand. 'The bureau?'
Yes. 'The drawer?' *Yes*
yes. We were so slow
bringing to light the yellowed
trove of albums: pressed
flower smiles of distant
aunts; old men who stared
as if they knew. 'You want
to look?' *No,* and a blunt
jab, *On the fire.* She spared
nobody, least of all
herself. That night
she died. Raking the grate
we salvaged one stiff curl
of silvery ash. Some quite
unknowable boy soldier's
face was ghosted there,
blacked up, benighted,
hair turned white
as zinc, like hers.

Rikki-Tikki-Tavi

A son of the Empire, fallen
    among Cornishmen,
    to a narrow one-
street village and a tribe of in-laws
    closed against you . . .
    Your colonial tan
soon bleached in the slatey rain.
    By the time I knew,
    you had shrunk away
as near invisible as flesh permits,
    the ghost of a military
    bearing. (No defence:
I wouldn't let you be, with my
    'But what *is* India?')

    Words, words
like *Bangalore, Madras.* The hiss
    like gas of Nag,
    king cobra.
Rikki-Tikki-Tavi juggling
    Nagaina's egg,
    an unexploded shell.
Your Gurkha *kukri.* ('Don't you tell
    Grandma I showed
    you this . . .')
The sip-sigh of a stainless blade
    from its scabbard.

'Did you fight?'
I stroked its edge. 'Did you *kill*?'
   Another long word –
   ceremonial . . .

which led you to Bombay,
   'a brave show',
   a bazaar of hooters
flags and bands, three cheers
   for a plucky mongoose
   mascot in the colours
as the troopship hauled away
   for France.

   They say
your face was one raw scar
   from mustard gas.

   I never saw.

The Ghost Trap

We climbed for weeks. After the armpit weather of
    Barrackpur
the air was like iced water: we were gasping, we were
gulping breaths that stung our throats, yet craving more.

Then the tree cover broke, and the clouds: first sight
of the mountains, ranged against us, the whole skyline
rucked, keen as if freshly broken, dangerously bright.

It flashed back our hearsay like a heliograph: *the Tsar's
agents in Lhasa . . . whispers in the Dalai Lama's ear . . .
moves in the Great Game . . . remember Kabul . . . ? the
    Afghan wars?*

We pushed closer, into the encirclement, crunching on ice-
locked screes that creaked under the weight of sunlight.
And we climbed. Once, in the shadow of a precipice

we saw a bright snow-flurry cresting from its lip. The track
was a rumour, all the gullies blind. Then deep in the rocks
a flicker and a drip alerted us. The stream ran on, not back.

We had crossed over. 'Hip hip . . .' I started. (I was young.)
No cheer came. The stillness was miles high. And a stone-
slip whispered. Echoes snickered round and round and on.

The word nobody breathed (yes, they remembered) was
    Kabul –
the expedition slaughtered, one man dragged home by his
    mule.
We eyed the overhangs, expecting the shot, the man-
    made rockfall

        for five days. *Chonk.*
    We wheeled. In the mist, *chonk*
chonk. We piled into cover just as something
        like a short-arsed cow
    botched out of greasy string
shambled by, its belled head bobbing. Now
        we saw the huts,
    a village slunk among boulders,
patched about with hides; no windows, no doors
        but a single hole
    where the smoke dribbled out,
where flat urchin faces peeped, then shrilled

and our way was blocked. Squat raggedy
bundles of men – were they men? –
swarmed and chittered. The Captain's voice
stayed them a moment; they faltered, then

flared. They were coming. At their head
a yappy pug-dog of a man, preposterous
with brass and bangles clanking, made
wild passes with an antique blunderbuss

[46]

and FIRE! the Captain gave the word.
The mob shuddered. They seemed to be
locked in a slow dance, swaying,
as the Maxim gun tracked patiently

back, forth, back. *So this is war,*
I thought dimly. *Why don't they run?*
Then their back rank broke. The crush
subsided with a groan. We hurried on.

And Lhasa? The Forbidden City was a slum.
        Sewers slopped the palace walls.
                His Most Serene
Magnificence, we were informed, was not at home.
        The Captain thundered our demands
                to underlings
who nodded and nodded and smiled. Why had we come,
        they asked, so laden and so far? Yes
                they would sign
a paper if it pleased us . . . And there was nothing
        more to say or stay for.
                As we turned
to go, one spoke in English. 'A question, sirs.
        What manner of being
                is a *Tsar*?'

We scoured the monastery for food.
No meat. Scrapings of meal.
It was a rat-run without corridors,
insulting sense as one bare cell
led to another, or a bare courtyard

or . . . Pungent nothingness. I stumbled,
cursed, then saw. It was a shrine
scabby with jewels. And there he was,
bunched in his robe. I'd never seen
a man so old, so utterly feeble.

He came straight at me. He was daft
with terror, brandishing this thing,
this . . . what? A rickety fly-swat
or a spider-web of sticks and string.
I stood, I almost laughed,

I was stern, I shouted, all
but wept. He would not stop.
When I pushed him he was light
as dust. He crumpled up
without a sound against the wall.

. . .

'GHOST TRAP (TIBET)'
                        It was in Tunbridge Wells,
some auction room. After fifty years, the very article!
I must have twitched. 'Sold to the Colonel,'

and the auctioneer came blathering like the fool
he is. 'Of course. Old India man like you.
Just up your street.' So here it is. No real value,

common as dirt out there, apparently. Do what you will
with it when I'm gone. But now? On the bedside table,
yes, within reach. Damned silly, isn't it? But still . . .

[48]

The Clever Children

'. . . the chicken or the egg?'
                              Their father
teased them on their way to bed.
They lay awake for hours, those clever
children. Then one little egghead said:

'Inside the shell, the embryonic hen's
got all her cells in her, even the cell
of *her* egg, within which . . . So on, in, on
in time, to the smallest conceivable!' Well,

now they *couldn't* sleep. They had to see
the ultimate egg, the egg of the future. On the way
how many breakages, unwanted omelettes, casually
discarded chickens? At last, there it lay

so tiny, so precious, so shimmeringly slight
it made them feel tremendous, like a pride
of giants. Now to sleep, but . . . 'Wait!'
said one (*yes*). 'What's *inside*?'

So they split it. What hatched out?
'Quick,' they yammered, 'put it back again.'
But those clever children couldn't, not
with all the king's horses, all the king's men.

Son and Heir

He's up. And off, a tipsy
    tightrope turn
juggling with gravity.
    The ascent of man
starts here. Like one spotlit

    he makes his stand
on the brink of a big-top
    drop. The ground
sways. One false step
    and . . .

Will he take it stonily
    like Sitting Bull?
Like holy Job? Or melancholy
    Charlie, fall-
guy to the old joke? Will he

    heck! He's baby-bald
Khrushchev, blamming a shoe
    on the diplomatic table –
'WE WILL BURY YOU . . .'

    No joke. He will.

Boys Fishing

He's got it, all the nonchalance
of a flick-knife. Ask his mates. What he wants

he wants. See how they turn to him.
He's snagged a gout of weed and swings it in

slap at their feet. They flinch
then scrum to see it twitch: a mud-green three-inch

crab that bridles free of weed,
huffs, bubbles at the sky and can't conceive

of such as him who casually ac-
curately heels his new black boot down *crack*.

It's mushed, still bubbling, legs awry,
as he turns back to his rod. Go on, ask him why.

'Cause I didn't want it.' Ten
years old, he is, and unassailable, and innocent.

A Chess Piece

Leather and ash, an old man's smell; sweat-
seasoned wood . . . They sit at prayer, at prey.
A hundred clocks tut-tut their precious time away
with choppers poised. This bloodless tête-à-tête

is called a Congress, but it's war: Versailles
nineteen-nineteen. Feeling the drag of history
the champion buckles to this season's prodigy,
a grave pale brat. The books hold no reply

to that blue-eyed, data-programmed innocence
(*Sometimes,* the mother says, *I wonder where he came*
from. He eats, sleeps and dreams the game . . .
Still, he's my boy.)
                    nor to the bleak Modern Defence –
king deeply bunkered, bishop in a fianchetto
sheathed in pawns, snug as a warhead in its silo.

The Cloud Chamber

for N.C. 1951–72

'You crack an atom, what's left? Particles,
bits. It's like Meccano: proton, neutron, quark.
Don't you see . . . ?'
                                    The things you knew.
The rest of us set our horizons at the girls'
school down the road. Whatever you
dreamed of, you left us in the dark.
('I couldn't follow him,' one friend confessed
after the fact, then *Why?* The waste, the waste!'
then again 'Did he *know* something we don't?')

'. . . there's nothing to it,' your pale face
lit on a smile. 'A molecule? A galaxy?
Nothing but little obstacles in space.'
As clear as mud. Just for a moment, though,
your laughter shook me. It was wild –
a touch of vertigo. I saw the solid world
come unput at our feet. I didn't see

the logic: how you would leave behind
friends, family, a fixed address,
even your books, until
                                    one tactful line
in the *Hatched-Matched-&-Despatched*: DIED
SUDDENLY. No note, no clue,
you left us nothing, as if we were less
than nothing (little obstacles?) to you.
'*Why?*' You'd have shrugged; worse, smiled.

[53]

'Why anything?' What could I say?
Except . . . that icy-crisp November night
we watched for meteors, crouched back to back
for warmth. 'There!'
                              'Where?'
                                            'Too late.'
A scatter-fall of debris from deep space.
I felt you shivering. I saw the track
in the cloud chamber. Bits. The waste.
The toll of microseconds. Particle decay.

Cloud chamber: *an apparatus in which the path of charged particles is made visible* (Chambers Dictionary)

A Civil Defence

'God forbid of course. But one must do *something*.' The
    Major
sighs: cloud-eyed from gin and ornithology, he's fuddled
by minutes-of-the-last, apologies, please-to-vacate-the-
    hall-
by-six (for the Brownies). He expands on Pascal's Wager.

'We assume Stinchfield survives. If not, well, we're dead.'
He mops his glasses. Flies zizz. Brown Owl taps the
    window.
'We must assume no radio, no telephone, no News At Ten,
    no
Epilogue. Imagine. *Someone* has to. Folk will have to be
    fed.

Tea urns: the WI should oblige. Water? I know a chap
who dowses. Livestock? I want a volunteer for sheep.
To count the blighters. Roughly. Mr Adams? Good. Keep
to the public footpaths, won't you? Anybody got a map?

Yes, just this parish. Then there's the Human Factor.
To identify the natural leaders . . . You know, captain
of the cricket team, so on. Also the bolshies. Jack Cane?
Yes, indeed. Then again, can anyone here mend a tractor?

Plus he has a shotgun. There may need to be . . . controls.
Survival of the fittest? Heavens, no! There'll be chaps'
    wives.
Miss Bundon for the playgroup. Doctor Crick. Mrs Troves
for her strawberry jam. And the vicar. There'll be souls

like swallows on the wires. Who'll tell them where to fly?'

Flying Dreams

PHILIP SMYTHE RADDALL, 'MISSING' 1943.

A dinky yellow dump-truck rusts
in brisk spring sun, up to its knees
in rubble and daisies. The straight thrust
   of a tarmac strip runs out
   to grass, an order countermanded
   suddenly, or overcome by doubt.
The outfield yawns, in service only
to be empty, stuck in a *drôle de guerre.*
The windsock wags its trunk in memory
   of braver days, whenever they were.
It points. It points to me.

There's a throat-clearing clatter, thinned
by distance, and a rickety single file
of trainers nudges out to sniff the wind,
   snub-nosed. They toe the line
   in cough-and-shuffle unison.
   One shudders and shifts; its whine
bites. And I'm hooked. The hop into flight
is nothing to that lift of pitch, that pulse,
that will to *go.* Going, gone, he's high
   off the edge of the hilltop; up he pulls
by his bootstraps into blustery bright

emptiness. And I've lost him. Phil,
it's you, boy uncle. It's your after-image
winking on an RAF-blue sky, the thrill
   of it, the pathos. Dreams. I grew
   up in your hand-me-downs, your shadow
   and your name. I ached to follow you.
At the Air Show, I decided to enlist.
I'd fly. But I was only six, and besides,
short-sighted.
                 Overhead an engine skips
   a beat; he's dipping back and rides
in as on surf. The undercarriage tips

turf and he flinches, doesn't slow
but bucks and revs again. (Somewhere
an officer's voice is crackling *No.*
   Again. Till it's perfect.) Lift,
   wingtips wobbling. He hops the hedge
   and away. I gasp. You'd have laughed:
*The flying's easy. It's the ground
that gets you in the end* . . . Yes,
other uncles, never you. No matter how
   they fade and fall to reminiscences
you won't come down, not now.

               *

    'Phil? One of the Few?
    Not him. No, Bomber Command.
    Ground crew.
    He never thought to fly

only they lost so many.
Tail-end Charlie on a Wellington.
Proud? He was twenty . . .'
As I take my leave

her eyes halt me: 'Tonight
as you walked in
I saw him, to the life.
Put you in uniform . . .'

Outside, I'm shivering: fight
or flight. There's the usual skyline
on the usual rust of light.
And suddenly, the moon.

*

Numb, effing
at the gut
gripe cold, bone
cracking din,
the cramp. No
where to look
but back. Slow
grey silk sea
in moon frost.
Then a blacked
out coastline
blotting foam
then

flak!

Ripped
glitter chills.
Then the shock
wave butts you.
Bastards!

Hung
in a steep
manoeuvre
you look down
where scattered
seeds bud flame
and blossom.
You smile.

Fire.
Fire! Fumble
with the gun.
Can't. Numb. Ice
bitches it.
(Night fighters
closing.) Ice
patterns craze
the glass. *Fire.*
But it feels
like ice.

                    Ten
            thousand dead
            in Hamburg.
            *(Do you read
            me? Do you
            read me?)* One
            boy 'missing'.
            Just a name.

                              *

Fire-storm: a brave new word.
Just drub enough bombs in
(we did it, Phil) and fire
feeds on itself, becomes it own
bellows and furnace. It was war,

it was orders, it was work well done.
Sleep, after all those long nights
waiting for the moon. Your ash sifts down
with dockers, mothers, dreaming Hitler brats.
It was Hamburg, it was Dresden,

a new world. We did it, Phil. Sleep
if you can. Will that blaze
smelt names, ranks, all our histories
together, till they lie at peace?

Sleep sound. I'll have the dreams.

Charlot's War

As the front falls back towards Armentières
the asylum keepers flit. Their charges, touched
or dumb, come out slowly, blinking. Where

is all the world going? What's this slow ruck
on the high road: bikes, prams, barrows stacked
with pots, pans, piglets, children? A khaki truck

blares. In the dust, a Madonna and Child in one,
Mimette rocks herself. Jean waves and grins. Charlot,
six-foot slab-featured farmer's son,

sees the ooze of fear made flesh. He bolts.
He's away across ploughed fields, ducking low
to the earth that smells of . . . what?

He forgets. Now he pants in a ditch. He slops
his face with scummy water, laps a bellyful
without mug or manners, then studies the plops

of small frogs for an hour. Upright again,
he finds a land that's no man's but his own.
Near by, a cow helves to a pitch of pain.

He smells milk frothed warm in a jug
and follows. But the farm is shuttered blind,
a trap: there's a whingeing snarl. A starved dog

dances on its rope like a baited bear. Run
Charlot run. The forest soothes him, but beyond
he drops, bristling. There's a wounded truck. Its man,

a soldier, bends beside it, thoughtfully
slashing each tyre, then beats each headlight in,
then unloads from the cab – Charlot cranes to see –

a wireless with a grinning dial and knobs like eyes –
Charlot gapes to hear – and with a pickaxe handle
crunches, then steps back, not feeling Charlot rise

behind him. Big hands clasp, and wring. Now mile
on mile Charlot stumbles and sobs. And there's
a cottage. He tires abruptly like a child

come home. It's almost welcoming the way the door
gives at one shove, into cool stale dark.
He wakes, hours later, on the parlour floor

to thunder, close. He creaks open the shutters.
Light catches an iron cage. He rips it. Three
canaries flop out. Two are dead. One flutters

weakly, crazily. He soothes it, sets it free.

A Mercy

Do something, she said.
                         The demolition
site had been a bomb blast in slow motion

and still smouldered. A faulty streetlamp
fizzled and pinked and – *there!* – that blank

rasp, clearly now: a cry about the size
and weight of a baby's. I picked and prised

among tipped slabs and shadows, till I saw
where it lay. I wrapped it gingerly. Indoors,

unswaddled, it curled and quivered. Fleas
snap-crackled in its spines. Leaves,

ash and clay crusted the lumpy bag
of a body that it somehow could not drag

as if I'd never freed it. Something inside
was crushed but not severed. And it cried.

DO something!
                         She watched as I filled
a rusty pail. I nudged it in. It scrabbled,

wallowed, useless. I rammed it under,
holding my own breath and holding, longer

than seemed possible, till with a shudder
it went slack. A silvery-quick globe of air

slipped from its mouth, broke surface
with a pock. I looked up. But her face

was turned away.

Clay

The potter's house grew from the soil it stands on,
thick cob walls slapped up from an oozy moat,
native clay.
        That week our children's wars
had their fortress and keep. A fringe of sycamores
walled out the miles beyond: their tonnage of wheat,
the air base with its mind turned east, the flat
horizons levelled by their own grey weight.

'Tonight we'll be firing.' Each cut of his spade
turned a gloss-tacky slab. The children bodged
glad shapes: 'Is that a bear?' 'Silly, it's you!'
His furnace champed our sticks and flushed and drew
one long huff. 'No smoke at this heat, no soot,'
he said. 'It's all consumed.' And he wedged
a chink open. I squinnied in. There they sat

in line, clod-faced homunculi, their silly
grins transfigured in the white-gold glare.
He bricked them in. We sat to watch the dark
come on. And suddenly a grid of steadier sparks
was moving through ours with a deep whining sigh –
a NATO bomber coming home to roost, so near,
so slow, we saw its engines with their tongues of fire.

. . .

and after all
has been unsaid,
undone: this . . .
Shall we say

the sea
is a black swag
of stage curtain
dropped in mid-act

and the spray's
wisht bloom
an after-image
of a great blaze

dancing,
that the wreck's
ribs sunk in sand
protect us

and the fire
where tar-blips
jig and squeal
on a driftwood griddle

centres all
on us like love?
Or shall we
hold our peace?

[67]

There is no sea
no shore
only this
you

me
after all this time
after all
this . . .

Outside in the dark
words founder
and those are not waves
that roar.